This book is a gift

from the

Lake County Public Library Foundation

Inside Special Operations

BRITISH ROYAL MARINES

Amphibious Division of
the United Kingdom's
Royal Navy

Bill Scheppler

the rosen publishing group's
rosen
central

F. St Andrews

Published in 2003 by The Rosen Publishing Group, Inc.
29 East 21st Street, New York, NY 10010

First Edition

Library of Congress Cataloging-in-Publication Data

Scheppler, Bill.
British Royal Marines: amphibious division of the United Kingdom's Royal Navy/By Bill Scheppler.—1st ed.
    v. cm.—(Inside special operations)
Includes bibliographical references and index.
Contents: A brief history of the British Royal Marines—Commando brigade Royal Marines—Commando support and specialist divisions—Commando weaponry and landing craft—Becoming a Royal Marines commando.
ISBN 0-8239-3806-9 (library binding)
1. Great Britain. Royal Marines—Juvenile literature. [1. Great Britain. Royal Marines. 2. Special forces (Military science)]
I. Title. II. Series.
VE57 .S34 2003
359.9'6'0941—dc21
                                                    2002009324

Manufactured in the United States of America

Contents

Royal Marines of Whisky Company 45 Commando prepare to board a Black Hawk helicopter in Afghanistan as part of Operation Buzzard. The Royal Marines set up roving vehicle checkpoints to search cars for weapons and suspected terrorists.

Introduction

*I'm profoundly grateful to the Royal Marines
for having made a man out of me.*

—Colonel Sam Basset, Royal Marines, 1907–1961

When he retired in 1961, Colonel Sam Basset ended a fifty-four-year career serving with the world's most respected military corps. He entered the Royal Marines as a fresh recruit, described by an early instructor as a "knock-kneed, pigeon-chested, flat-footed bloody waste of a uniform!" He left as a shrewd, battle-tested leader respected equally by superiors and subordinates alike—a living legend.

The remarkable length of Colonel Basset's career and the amount of success he enjoyed as a Royal Marine are unusual feats indeed. However, the personal transformation he experienced along the way is repeated year after year in the new recruits who enter basic training and emerge thirty weeks later sporting the Green Beret of the Royal Marines Commandos.

British Royal Marines don the coveted Green Beret with all the honor and respect due the world's longest-standing special operations (special ops) force. In Great Britain and around the globe, those who wear the Green Beret represent the qualities of the spirit: leadership; unselfishness; cheerfulness under adversity; courage and determination; and high professional standards. It has become a symbol of Britain's heroic past, valiant present, and determined future.

Royal Marines have been on active duty for more than 335 years, and they remain an influential force in today's international affairs. Currently deployed on operations around the world, Royal Marines are taking part most notably in peace-keeping and antiterrorist missions in Afghanistan, the Persian Gulf, and other hotbeds of military activity.

The Royal Marines continue to be relevant in the modern world because they are expert at adapting to the needs of an ever-changing global landscape. From "sea soldiers" to commandos, over the past three centuries Royal Marines have evolved from sailors who could fight on land to an elite force that can fight anywhere. And today's Royal Marines do much more than fight. In addition to combat, Royal Marines play an important role in humanitarian, policing, and conflict resolution efforts around the world.

The best of the best, the Royal Marines Commando units that emerged to launch daring, specialized assault raids against Nazi troops during World War II set the standard for all special operations forces to follow. Royal Marines continue to lead the way in areas of strategy, technology, and training, yet the corps remains steeped in history and tradition. Royal Marines wear their legend on their uniforms in the form of badges displaying the official corps insignia.

Six respected symbols make up the Royal Marines crest, each unique in significance and design, detailing three centuries of service to the Crown.

The Royal Marines crest combines six symbols key to Britain's Crown.

- Displayed prominently atop the crest, **the lion and the crown** form a time-honored British symbol, which identifies the corps as a royal regiment.

In 1802, following the French Revolution, King George III presented this honor to the Royal Marines in recognition of their exemplary service.

- The word **"Gibraltar"** appears on a banner just below the crown, immortalizing the heroic 1704 battle that resulted in the capture and defense of the Rock of Gibraltar. King George IV considered this event to be one of the Royal Marines' greatest achievements.

- In 1827, King George IV replaced individual battle honors with a **globe**, acknowledging corps victories in every quarter of the world.

- The addition of the **laurels** salutes the particularly valiant efforts of the Royal Marines during the 1762 capture of Belle Isle.

- A **fouled anchor** (tangled with rope), positioned under the globe where the laurels meet, is the traditional badge of the lord high admiral and signifies the Royal Marines' place within the Royal Navy. This symbol was added to the crest in 1747.

- The Royal Marines motto, *Per Mare Per Terram*, which is Latin for "by sea by land," appears on a ribbon at the bottom of the crest. Although it is not certain exactly when the motto was adopted, it appeared as early as the Battle of Bunker Hill in 1775 during the American Revolution.

Of course, the history behind these symbols, while impressive and worthy of admiration, barely scratches the surface of the myriad honors and accomplishments earned by the Royal Marines over the decades. Nevertheless, no other military unit wears its badge with more pride.

This book attempts to do some justice to the legend and tradition of the British Royal Marines. It begins with a brief history of the corps and descriptions of its primary and supporting divisions. You will read about the weaponry and vehicles employed by the corps. Finally, you will learn what it takes to become a Royal Marines Commando and what the near future may hold for this elite special ops force.

1. A Brief History of the British Royal Marines

The British Royal Marines are the amphibious division of the United Kingdom's Royal Navy. For more than 300 years, this special operations unit has set the standard for excellence, preparedness, and valor in the face of battle. Royal Marines have played an active role in military campaigns around the globe, going back to the late seventeenth century. They are widely respected as being among history's best-trained armed forces.

An amphibious military division is one that is equally capable on land or at sea. In 1664, the Royal Navy was a strong, international military force, but it was capable of engaging the enemy only at sea—in ship-to-ship or ship-to-land combat—which greatly limited its effectiveness. At that time, the duke of York, serving as the lord high admiral of the Royal Navy, commissioned 1,200 recruits to be trained as foot soldiers in addition to their standard seamen instruction. These multidisciplined soldiers were deployed among British warships, and the marines were born.

The Royal Marines have evolved greatly since their formation, and in fact there are more differences than similarities between that first batch of recruits and the highly specialized Royal Marines Commandos of today. Although sharing the same amphibious beginnings, modern Royal Marines Commandos operate on land, at sea, and even in the air. They are trained to perform in any environment, from the icy mountains of northern Europe to the sultry jungles of the Far East.

The Origin of the Royal Marines

Being an island nation, England has always relied heavily upon maritime defenses for its survival. Its powerful naval fleets, waging war in the waters surrounding the British Isles, fought off would-be invaders from setting foot on British soil for hundreds of years. Equally as important, the deployment of armed ships to escort cargo vessels against the threat of seafaring pirates was instrumental in protecting the United Kingdom's vital shipping trade.

By the 1600s, the Royal Navy was already regarded as one of the world's most powerful fleets, having defeated the mighty Spanish Armada—141 ships strong, transporting 7,500 sailors and over 20,000 troops—in its attempt to invade England in 1588. Despite this success, the seventeenth century saw a reduction in the number of vessels composing the Royal Navy. The emergence of massive new gunboats, such as the *Sovereign of the Seas*, proved that a smaller fleet could be equally effective. Commissioned by Charles I in 1637, the *Sovereign of the Seas* was the most powerful warship in the water, boasting 102 cannons on three decks.

Gibraltar

The word "Gibraltar" appears on the official Royal Marines badge in remembrance of one of their most valiant triumphs. In 1704, during war with France and Spain, a combined force of British and Dutch marines captured the Rock of Gibraltar and held their ground under siege for eight months. At one point during the campaign, 17 Royal Marines faced off against 500 French troops and defended their position against multiple assaults.

On October 28, 1664, toward the beginning of the second Anglo-Dutch War (a naval campaign between England and the Netherlands), the duke of York assembled a group of "sea soldiers," initially labeled the Duke of York and Albany's Maritime Regiment of Foot, or the Admiral's Regiment. This 1,200-strong unit was divided into six companies and immediately began preparing for a new, amphibious style of combat.

The Maritime Regiment of Foot saw its first action in July 1667. Upon landing 3,000 troops at Harwich, England, the Dutch split off one

During the Battle of Lowestoft, the Admiral's Regiment defended English soil by blowing up the flagship of the Dutch.

company and marched to Landguard Fort, which was simultaneously under siege by Dutch gunboats off the coast. Two companies of the Admiral's Regiment engaged the Dutch soldiers and made quick work of the invaders. After regrouping and forging a second assault the next day, the Dutch were again repelled by the sea soldiers. This was to be the first and last time the regiment would engage an enemy on English soil, and the gallantry shown in that encounter remains at the heart of the Royal Marines' reputation to this day.

This is a private of the Royal Marines. From early on, the Royal Marines worked with both the army and the admiralty.

Organizational Evolution

Over the next 100 years, the Royal Marines were disbanded and reformed multiple times as the need for their services—and the military budget required to fund them—fluctuated. From its inception, the regiment was under the control of the admiralty when at sea and the army when on land. But in 1755, during a buildup for war with France, the admiralty folded them entirely into its organization, and the Royal

Marines have remained an active division of the Royal Navy ever since.

During the nineteenth century and the early part of the twentieth century, Royal Marines participated in military campaigns around the world. Among other locations, they fought in West Africa during the Seven Years' War; served in Hong Kong during the capture of Canton; battled in the Ukraine during the Crimean War; and waged multiple air, land, and sea raids throughout World War I.

Their duties were to act as sharpshooters and gunners on ship; join boarding parties in the seizure of enemy vessels; occupy captured fortresses until relieved by the army; and, when necessary, engage in land battles and assaults. But a dramatic change in the role of the Royal Marines was only around the corner. In 1942, the first commando unit was formed, which would forever change the role of the Royal Marines and pave the way for the special operations experts we know them to be today.

Enter the Royal Marines Commando

The advent of military air power, most notably the infamous German blitzkrieg style of sustained bombing, changed the face of warfare in World War II. Naval power remained important, especially in blocking shipping lines to deny the enemy from obtaining incoming resources. But for the first time, an invading power could avoid direct confrontation with the Royal Navy by flying above it and attacking England directly from the skies.

As the invading German army rolled across Europe, England looked increasingly like a sitting duck. The need to take an offensive role became apparent, and the country called on the Royal Marines to provide the grit and muscle needed to get the job done.

British Royal Marines prepare for the Allied forces' invasion of Normandy by conducting a mock assault on a North African beach.

Britain's prime minister Winston Churchill declared, in 1940, a need for "specially trained troops of the hunter class, who can develop a reign of terror down on these [enemy occupied] coasts." The military embraced Churchill's mandate, and two years later, the first Royal Marines Commando unit was engaged in action. By 1944, their numbers swelled to nine units.

On June 6, 1944, Britain and the Allies launched Operation Overlord, a pivotal assault on the beaches of Normandy, in an effort to gain a foothold into Nazi-occupied France. Sixteen thousand Royal Marines took part in the campaign, manning two-thirds of the landing craft, and commando units were some of the first to land and fight. After enduring impossible hardship, the troops helped to establish a beachhead, which would prove to be a mortal blow to the German army and a turning point in the war.

After World War II, Britain realized that in a fast-evolving world, small bands of elite soldiers could be as valuable as entire infantry divisions. As a result, every Royal Marines recruit since 1945—with the exception of the Royal Marines Band Service—has been required to complete commando training.

2. 3 Commando Brigade Royal Marines

In the decades since World War II, the Royal Marines earned a reputation as one of the world's best-prepared special operations groups, and along the way, the organization evolved into today's streamlined outfit. From a peak of 80,000 during World War II, fewer than 8,000 troops make up today's Royal Marines corps, and at the heart is 3 Commando Brigade Royal Marines (3 Cdo Bde RM).

3 Cdo Bde RM comprises three divisions: 40 Commando Royal Marines, 42 Commando Royal Marines, and 45 Commando Royal Marines. Each division boasts over 600 men and is subdivided into six companies based on concentrations such as

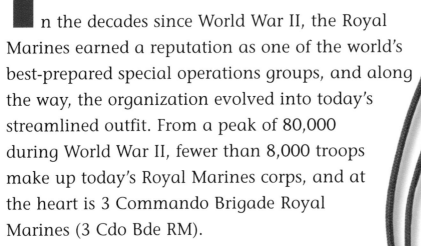

logistics and close combat. Although 3 Cdo Bde RM divisions are headquartered in England, individual units are stationed in locations around the world and remain in a constant state of readiness. This enables Royal Marines Commandos to be deployed anywhere on Earth within twenty-four hours, adding immediate combat capability to an already daunting arsenal.

All three commando divisions have direct roots in the pioneering brigades of the Second World War and share a high standard of training and aptitude that has remained virtually unchanged for generations. Troops are deployed in many different configurations, from small bands of commandos to entire companies, to engage any enemy that threatens the vital security interests of Britain and her allies.

40 Commando Royal Marines

40 Commando Royal Marines has a distinguished sixty-year history, dating back to February 14, 1942, when the first Royal Marines Commando unit (originally labeled "A" Commando) was introduced.

Only six months after its formation, 40 Commando entered World War II in Operation Jubilee, on August 18, 1942, in a raid by Allied forces on the German army occupying Dieppe, France. Operation Jubilee was not a success, but 40 Commando

These soldiers returning from Operation Jubilee in Dieppe, France, were part of the largest combined operations raid ever. The raid included special troops from the United Kingdom, France, Canada, and the United States.

turned things around during action in the Italian Campaign from 1943 to 1945. The unit was instrumental in a decisive victory over the Germans in the Battle for Termoli and later in the taking of Lake Comacchio, which paved the way for an amphibious attack and the eventual Nazi retreat from Italy.

Immediately following World War II, 40 Commando played an important role as rearguard for the British protectorate in Palestine. The protectorate paved the way for today's state of Israel, which was founded following the British military's pullout in 1948.

In subsequent decades, 40 Commando played a security role in regions of British interest, such as Hong Kong, Cyprus, and

Egypt. The unit spent much of the 1960s stationed in Singapore, where it was deeply involved in the Indonesian confrontation initiated by Brunei rebels over the foundation of Malaysia.

During the 1982 Falkland Islands War, 40 Commando troops were among the first ashore at Ajax Bay in San Carlos, Argentina, as part of Operation Corporate. The three-week campaign collapsed enemy resistance, ultimately leading to the Argentineans' surrender.

In 1983, 40 Commando moved into its current head-quarters at Norton Manor Camp, near Taunton in the southwest of England. The division spent a busy decade in the 1990s, undertaking its first-ever deployment to Norway, a stint in Iraq during the Gulf War, and tours of duty in Northern Ireland, the Asia-Pacific rim, and the Congo in Africa.

A British Royal Marine guards captured Argentine soldiers during the Falkland Islands War.

42 Commando Royal Marines

42 Commando Royal Marines was introduced in 1943. The creation of 42 Commando led to the practice of grouping commando units into brigades, which in turn produced the formation of 102 Royal Marines Brigade—later renamed 3 Commando Brigade Royal Marines—thus establishing the organization that stands today.

42 Commando is headquartered in Bickleigh Barracks, in Plymouth, England. Bickleigh has a colorful past, having served as a sewage disposal farm, a World War II refugee camp, and Royal Marines training school, among other purposes. 42 Commando overtook the facility in 1971 to take advantage of its exemplary training ranges and favorable coastal access.

Royal Marines Band Service

Music and the military have always gone hand in hand, from soldiers marching to the beat of a drum to the sound of a bugler blowing "Reveille" as a wake-up call to the troops. Today's Royal Marines Band Service provides a wide range of band styles including orchestras, marching bands, and dance bands. As highly trained as the commandos, band service members must also pass demanding physical tests and weapons training.

During the 1950s, 42 Commando saw action in the Korean War and the Lebanon crisis, and it provided the initial landing force on the beaches of Port Said in the Suez crisis. In 1960, the division was assigned to HMS *Bulwark,* a former aircraft carrier that had been converted into a commando carrier. The *Bulwark* landed 42 Commando units in Kuwait during Operation Vantage to play a role in protecting Kuwait from Iraqi invasion.

45 Commando Royal Marines

Formed in August 1943, 45 Commando Royal Marines saw plenty of action in the final years of World War II. The division participated in the D-Day landings at Normandy and was involved in the crossings of the Rhine, Weser, and Elbe Rivers during Operation Market Garden.

45 Commando continued to be active following World War II. In November 1956, during the Suez crisis, it took part in the first-ever operational helicopter assault—500 men from 45 Commando were airlifted from the HMS *Ocean* and the HMS *Theseus* and transported near Port Said, where they executed the triumphant takeover of Gamil Airfield. The success of this convinced the Royal Navy to convert the *Bulwark* into a full-time commando carrier, housing helicopters exclusively instead of fixed-wing aircraft.

A Royal Marine stationed near the Arctic Circle wears a white-taped helmet and a white face mask as camouflage. The 45 Commando was the first division to specialize in cold weather warfare.

In 1971, after a quarter century of operational service abroad, 45 Commando moved into its current headquarters at Royal Marines Condor, Arbroath, on Scotland's eastern coast. Located in a more frigid climate, 45 Commando was the first 3 Cdo Bde RM division to specialize in mountain and cold weather warfare. The unit established amphibious training north of the Arctic Circle and was soon deployed to defend Norway and the North Atlantic Treaty Organization's (NATO) northern flank.

In a heroic effort during the Falkland Islands War, 45 Commando successfully defeated Argentinean forces in the pivotal battle for Two Sisters Mountain on the island of East Falkland. The unit has actually seen increased activity in the post–Cold War era. In 1991, 45 Commando served on humanitarian assistance

Operation Snipe

In April and May 2002, 45 Commando was deployed to Afghanistan to participate in Operation Snipe, a seek-and-destroy mission intended to clear a mountainous area of terrorists' bunkers, weapons caches, and other fortifications. The operation was a success, resulting in the destruction of a sizable cache and the securing of defensive positions, paving the way for humanitarian aid to civilians living in the war-torn region.

duty in northern Iraq, returning to the Middle East in 1994 to reinforce the Kuwaiti border against Iraqi aggression. The unit has also conducted a variety of missions in locations such as Nicaragua, Belize, and Kosovo between the years 1998 and 2000.

Effective as it can be when operating on its own, 3 Cdo Bde RM has an important support system available through other divisions of England's military forces. When teamed with members of this support system, commandos become more self-contained, more mobile, and an all-around more capable force.

3. Commando Support and Specialist Divisions

The 3 Commando Brigade Royal Marines Corps is the core of today's Royal Marines organization, but it is a diverse corps that can be deployed in a number of different configurations based on the assigned task. In addition to its own commando specialist divisions, the Royal Marines have a wide variety of support groups from which to draw upon, including the Royal Navy, the British Army, the Royal Air Force, and the Royal Fleet Auxiliary.

When commandos and supporting units are assembled together for deployment, the team is referred to as an amphibious ready group (ARG). An ARG can be a completely self-contained unit, surviving for weeks or months without a fixed base—even without solid ground—allowing the team to lay in wait indefinitely and to attack undetected. An ARG may contain specialist artillery units for increased firepower, engineers to perform tasks such as demolitions and minesweeping, and logistical regiments responsible for combat support, such as setting up temporary command posts and medical facilities.

With the Royal Marines Commandos regarded among the world's best-trained soldiers, commando specialist divisions are elevated to the elite of the elite. Specialist divisions such as the Special Boat Squadron, Mountain and Arctic Warfare Cadre, and 539 Assault Squadron focus their training on specific, highly demanding skills. Their expertise greatly enhances the potency of any assault team to which they are assigned. This chapter takes a closer look at the three main commando specialist divisions and their unique abilities.

Special Boat Squadron

Like the commandos themselves, specialist units such as the Special Boat Squadron (SBS) have their roots in World War II. These small bands of highly trained marines were formed to conduct advance reconnaissance operations and carry out covert raiding missions that could only be executed by a handful of men equipped with the latest weapons and technology.

After the war, many specialist units were disbanded, but the division that would become the SBS continued as the Small Raids Wing of the Royal Marines Amphibious School. This group, whose members are referred to as "swimmer-canoeists," served in the Korean War working closely with 45 Commando. They earned their official name in 1977 after thirty years of consistently holding up their impossibly high standard of service.

The SBS is based at Poole, in the southwestern county of Dorset, although individual units are stationed worldwide. Swimmer-canoeists played a major role during the Falkland Islands War as the first group to land ashore on South Georgia Island. In dramatic fashion, the unit flew from England to the South Atlantic region, where they parachuted into the frigid

29 Commando

When 3 Cdo Bde RM needs firepower, it calls on 29 Commando of the British Army. 29 Commando boasts massive weapons such as 105 mm light guns and 120 mm mortars, which can be used to take out enemy defenses and clear a safer path for assault raids. 29 Commando units complete the Royal Marines Commando course and don the coveted Green Beret.

ocean and boarded a British submarine. From there, they worked closely with units from the Special Air Service (SAS) to provide recon support for the larger beach landings.

In peacetime, the SBS stays busy with deployments in Northern Ireland, the defense of NATO's northern flank in Norway, protection of Britain's offshore oil interests, and training exercise and development with the U.S. Navy SEALs and the Royal Netherlands Marines.

Mountain and Arctic Warfare Cadre

An essential part of 3 Cdo Bde RM, the Mountain and Arctic Warfare (M&AW) Cadre is a commando specialist division that concentrates on ski, mountain, and winter warfare. The demands of working in these harsh conditions require a training program that is second to none, and the yearlong course to become a "mountain leader" is exactly that.

Recruits into the M&AW Cadre are commandos that have already served in 3 Cdo Bde RM for several years. These superbly conditioned soldiers are put through a series of exercises during which they learn to climb, ski, survive, and fight in some of the world's most challenging environments. Like marines in the other commando specialist divisions, they become expert snipers and parachutists. Unlike the

Royal Marines from the M&AW (Mountain and Arctic Warfare) Cadre train in the French Alps by climbing a mountain covered in snow and ice. M&AW Cadre soldiers must be able to navigate rough terrain in harsh weather conditions while carrying out regular special operations duties.

other specialists, they must pass a sequence of tactical drills designed for harsh subzero conditions, including a two-week exercise in the mountains of Norway in the dead of winter. The severity of the training program becomes apparent when you consider that nearly 80 percent of M&AW Cadre hopefuls do not pass the first time around.

The M&AW Cadre is responsible for testing most of the new equipment developed for British troops in the Arctic, which means they are always equipped with the latest technology and weaponry. A mountain leader looks like a character from a sci-fi movie, skiing down a snow-capped mountain, dressed in white from head to toe, and carrying his pack with an SA-80 rifle slung across his back. However, with experience, a member of the M&AW Cadre will tell you that it is actually easier to ski with all that equipment than to march on foot, as most other soldiers are required to do.

539 Assault Squadron

One of the youngest units in the British military, 539 Assault Squadron was formed in the wake of the Falkland Islands War. This specialist division provides expert landing craft, raiding craft, and hovercraft capabilities for 3 Cdo Bde RM. It deploys boat groups for operations worldwide and provides increased mobility to the force. The unit's number was taken from the Royal Navy's most honored landing craft fleet to take part in the D-Day invasion of Normandy.

Prior to the Falklands conflict, the Royal Navy managed all sea vessels, while the Royal Marines Landing Craft Branch supplied the crews, and the Royal Marines Raiding Squadrons provided the amphibious soldiers. During the war, the Landing Craft Branch and Raiding Squadrons came together to form an independent Royal Marines amphibious squadron, which did not need to rely on the Royal Navy to deploy its troops. In April 1984, 539 Assault Squadron Royal Marines (ASRM) was established.

All members of 539 ASRM are commandos before joining the squadron. After a four-week course in seamanship, a soldier enters the squadron at the rank of coxswain LC 3. This grade allows the commando to crew a landing craft, but the LC 3 must serve for over a year in this role before he may be considered to take part in the ten-week LC 2 training program. It is only after passing this highly concentrated course that the commando earns the opportunity to command a Royal Marines landing craft.

Commando
4. Weaponry and Landing Craft

In order to achieve their objectives of mobility and stealth, Royal Marines Commandos embark on raids and other deployments carrying only the bare essentials of equipment. This normally limits their munitions to lightweight weapons such as rifles, submachine guns, grenades, and demolition charges; but what the commandos lack in firepower, they make up for in precision and strategy.

3 Cdo Bde RM does not operate a wide variety of motor vehicles. Aside from getting troops into and out of combat zones, vehicles serve little purpose in commando

operations. The aquatic landing craft operated by 539 Assault Squadron and a relatively small number of helicopters serve the brigade's deployment needs, but the Royal Marines rely on the Royal Navy for ocean transport and the British Army for the majority of its land-based vehicles.

Because commando armament can vary from mission to mission and the brigade relies heavily on its support groups for additional weaponry and transportation needs, it is difficult to cover all of the equipment employed by a commando unit. Add to that the fact that the Royal Marines are constantly testing the latest technology, and it becomes almost impossible. But to give you an idea of the resources available to commandos in the line of duty, this chapter describes the standard firepower and landing craft used by the Royal Marines Commandos today.

SA-80 Assault Rifle

Some divisions within the British armed forces substitute the SA-80 for the M16, and the Mountain and Arctic Warfare Cadre is one of them. At 5.56 mm, the caliber of the SA-80 is identical to the M16, but the more compact design of the SA-80 makes it easier to carry and operate for mountain leaders, who are loaded down with additional harsh-weather equipment

Weapons

Commando units are usually lightly armed. Their need to move quickly under their own power eliminates the option of carrying heavy weapons or large numbers of smaller arms. Commando training, however, includes familiarity with all weapon types, which enables the commando to use any enemy weapon that may fall into his hands. A selection of standard issue Royal Marines weapons are listed and described below.

L9A1 9 mm automatic pistol Commonly known as the Browning 9 mm or Browning Hi-Power, this 9 mm automatic pistol has been the sidearm of choice for the Royal Marines since the Second World War. Its thirteen-round magazine capacity is large for this class, and its long grip ensures a steady aim. The Browning 9 mm is effective up to 55 yards (50.3 meters).

M16A2 5.56 mm semiautomatic rifle The M16 or Armalite is one of the world's most popular military weapons. It can fire up to sixty rounds per minute with an effective range of over 400 yards (approximately 366 meters). Commandos can attach the M203 grenade launcher to this weapon and fire a variety of 40 mm projectiles, including tear gas and smoke canisters.

MP5 9 mm submachine gun The latest submachine gun to be employed by the Royal Marines, the MP5 combines a lightweight weapon with adequate range and is capable of firing off 800 rounds per minute. Accessories such as laser sights and noise dampers are easily fastened to this versatile and popular weapon.

L7A2 7.62 mm general purpose machine gun (GPMG) The GPMG is a large and heavy machine gun that requires two soldiers to operate: the shooter and the loader. Steps have been taken to abandon this gun in favor of lighter weapons, but sometimes there is just no substitute for a fire rate of 1,000 rounds per minute.

L96A1 7.62 mm sniper rifle Designed for precise, long-distance shooting, the L96 is accurate enough to achieve a first-round hit at more than 900 yards (around 823 meters) and can be effective beyond 1,200 yards (1,097 meters). Although fully adjustable iron sights for use to 750 yards (686 meters) are standard, the rifle is routinely upgraded with a telescopic sight.

L16 81 mm mortar A light and versatile weapon, this projectile is so effective at over 5,500 yards (5,030 meters) that the British military ultimately rejected heavier mortars in favor of a higher volume of L16 ammunition. Commandos also use a much lighter but equally efficient 51 mm mortar.

MILAN shoulder-launched anti-tank weapon The MILAN consists of two main components, the launcher and the missile, clipped together to prepare the system for use. On firing, the operator needs only to keep his aiming mark on the target and the SACLOS (semi-automatic command to line of sight guidance system) does the rest.

94 mm light anti-tank weapon (LAW94) A one-shot, disposable rocket launcher, the LAW94 is lightweight enough to allow a single commando to engage an enemy tank at a range of more than 545 yards (498 meters). Due to the low cost of the LAW94, each commando unit is equipped with 100 of these advanced weapon systems.

Vehicles

From the 100-ton capacity LCU to the two-person collapsible Klepper canoe, Royal Marines Commandos have a wide range of waterborne craft to draw on for amphibious landings. In recent years, however, helicopter deployment has become an increasingly common method of positioning commando troops. The following landing craft and helicopters are most frequently used for commando transport.

Landing craft unit Mark 4 (LCU). The purpose of the LCU is to deliver large vehicles and/or large numbers of marines from ship to shore. These vessels are almost 30 yards (27.4 meters) in length, have a range of over 200 nautical miles, and can transport 100 tons of cargo at speeds up to 10 knots.

Landing craft vehicle and personnel Mark 5 (LCVP) With a capacity of thirty-five troops and their equipment or two light trucks, the LCVP is a smaller and faster landing craft for use in mid-size operations. The Mark 5 is the latest generation LCVP. Commissioned in 2001 and not yet available, it will have a top speed of 24 knots.

Rigid raiding craft Mark 3 (RRC) The Rigid Raider is the classic commando landing craft. Quiet and sleek, these modest looking vessels are unsinkable and can unload a team of eight commandos with little or no enemy detection. Quick when it needs to be, the RRC can reach speeds of 30 to 35 knots.

British Royal Marines from 40 Commando carry out an amphibious landing, part of an exercise to train the Royal Marines for use as ground forces in Afghanistan.

Inflatable raiding craft Mark 2 (IRC) Another landing craft option for small raiding teams is the IRC. Although its capacity is limited to five commandos and their gear, the IRC is portable and resilient. Its rigid inflatable hull is even less susceptible to certain types of damage than the Rigid Raider.

Sea King Mark 4 The Sea King support helicopter has a 6,000-pound lift capacity, giving it the ability to carry up to twenty-seven troops or sixteen fully equipped comman-dos. Depending on the load, which may include 105 mm guns or light trucks slung underneath, the Mark 4 can travel a distance of 400 to 600 miles (644–966 kilometers).

Lynx AH Mark 7 The Lynx doubles as a landing craft and a light attack helicop-

Royal Marines from 40 Commando huddle in front of a Royal Navy Sea King helicopter. The British Royal Marines rely on the Royal Navy for ocean transport and the British Army for most land transport.

ter. This aircraft can deploy a team of up to ten commandos, but it is also an effective antitank weapon. The Mark 7 features a tube-launched optically tracked wire-guided (TOW) missile system, which can penetrate the hulls of every known battle tank.

Enter the Hippo

After forty years of loyal service, the Royal Marines are ready to phase out the CeBARV in favor of a modern beach recovery vehicle. The "Hippo" future beach recovery vehicle (FBRV) is currently undergoing operational testing, and the first four units are scheduled for arrival in 2002–2003. Improvements to the FBRV weight distribution, gear ratio, and suspension give the Hippo greater traction and pushing power.

Land Rover trucks The Royal Marines employ 1/2-ton, 3/4-ton, and 1-ton Land Rovers for appropriate transport needs. The 1/2-ton and 3/4-ton trucks generate identical horsepower output, so the lighter 1/2-ton is used extensively on maneuvers, while the 3/4-ton plays the role of supply truck. Thanks to its considerable power and hauling capacity, the 1-ton sees a good deal of action, often loaded with large 105 mm guns or 81 mm mortar teams.

Centurion beach armored recovery vehicle (CeBARV) Armed with a 7.62 mm machine gun and 650 horsepower, the primary purpose of the CeBARV is to assist stranded vehicles during amphibious operations. First used by the Royal Marines in 1962, this track-propelled vehicle can function in up to ten feet of water.

5. Becoming a Royal Marines Commando

Immediately after a Royal Marine completes his basic training, he is ready to be deployed for military action anywhere in the world. The thirty-week commando training program is known to be one of the world's longest and most demanding. But exactly what happens during those seven months spent at the Commando Training Center Royal Marines (CTCRM) that turns regular citizens into elite soldiers?

It all begins with the most promising recruits. In order to be eligible to join the Royal Marines, a prospective recruit must be a British citizen between the ages of seventeen and twenty-eight. But these requirements do not automatically guarantee admission into the CTCRM. The first stage in becoming a commando is the Potential Royal Marines Course (PRMC): a three-day trial during which potential recruits get a taste of CTCRM life. The PRMC is largely informational, but recruits must exhibit top physical condition, since their strength, stamina, and determination will be tried in a series of challenging tests. Only recruits who pass the PRMC are eligible for Royal Marines basic training.

The commando training program is arranged into seven modules that combine to form an operational performance standard (OPS), which is consistent across all Royal Marines from recruits to reservists to officers. This standardization is unique to the Royal Marines and has become a cornerstone of success,

Trial by Fire

In 1991, during Operation Desert Storm, Royal Marines Commandos were deployed to Iraq as part of Operation Haven. While this deployment was under way, a class of marines and officers passed out of CTCRM and immediately received orders to join the operation. The commandos literally graduated from basic training on a Friday and flew to northern Iraq the following day.

ensuring that all personnel are equally capable in infantry skills and ultimately strengthening the commando spirit.

Training Phase I

Training begins the moment a new troop of recruits steps off the bus at CTCRM. A troop may consist of up to fifty-five men, but it is likely to shrink as the training wears on and recruits drop out. The purpose of Phase I is to assimilate the recruits into the Royal Marines lifestyle and prepare them physically and mentally for the demands in Phase II.

Foundation (weeks 1–3) Beginning with the most basic exercises, the Foundation module introduces civilians to the military. Recruits receive their first military haircuts, learn to make their beds properly and keep their gear clean, and begin to march and drill. Physical training starts immediately, and recruits are regularly tested for performance. Foundation culminates with First Step, a twenty-four-hour exercise during which recruits master the basics of living in the field.

Individual skills training (weeks 4–10) This module teaches basic infantry skills such as weapons handling and maintenance, camouflage, and map reading, and eventually night movement, target indication, stalking, and more. These abilities are vital in the Marshall Star and Hunter's Moon exercises, when night sentry, navigation, and concealment skills are tested. Recruits spend hours in the classroom studying the theory behind these skills before exercising them in the field.

Advanced skills training (weeks 10–15) The final module of Phase I has the recruits going up in their first helicopter exercise, throwing their first live grenades, and building survival shelters. By now, recruits should be comfortable living in the field and handling weapons, and the final exercise is their chance to prove it. Baptist Run is a culmination of all skills learned up to this point. The thirty-two-hour test in the field determines whether or not a recruit has the knowledge and determination to advance to Phase II.

Training Phase II

Armed with basic combat skills, recruits are introduced to realistic deployment scenarios in Training Phase II. These exercises test the recruits' abilities and further develop their physical conditioning. The final tests on the commando course and graduation at the end of week thirty stand out as Phase II highlights.

Operations of War Training (weeks 16–23) In this module, recruits encounter several wartime exercises, from basic patrolling in First Base to ambushes and recon in Second

Empire and village defense in Violent Entry. At the same time, they are introduced to battle physical training (BPT), which includes an assault course and twelve-mile (about nineteen-kilometer) marches with seventy-pound (almost thirty-two-kilogram) packs.

Commando course (weeks 24–26) This module focuses on verifying that recruits can perform at a commando level of fitness. Recruits are introduced to the courses that make up the commando tests, which they will be required to pass at the end of the module. In the meantime, they undergo amphibious training in the Sudden Jab exercise and learn vertical assault techniques from mountain leaders.

Royal Marines from 45 Commando carry out gun drills during training in Oman. The marines are using .5 Browning machine guns in this exercise.

Professional training (weeks 27–29) The professional training module contains the last exercise, Final Thrust, which replicates the conditions of war and forces recruits to utilize every skill developed over the previous twenty-eight weeks. Combining boat landings, raids, helicopter deployments, night assaults, and large quantities of nerve-racking live ammunition, this exercise demands teamwork and courage under stark adversity.

King's Squad (week 30) The final module is a preparatory week for King's Squad Pass Out Day. Recruits fine-tune their parade and drill display and complete administrative requirements to clear the way for their first official deployment. Dressed in their best blue uniforms, at pass out recruits receive the coveted Green Beret of the Royal Marines Commando and become members of history's most revered military corps.

The Commando Tests

The Royal Marines commando tests are legendary for the overwhelming demands they place on Royal Marines recruits. Commandos are among the best soldiers in the world because of their consistent valor on the battlefield, but they are the best-trained because they have passed the commando tests. The tests are a series of four physical fitness assessments, which must be attempted and passed during a three-day stretch in week twenty-six.

Endurance course The endurance course is a six-mile ordeal that combines a two-mile obstacle course with a four-mile run, while hauling over thirty pounds of gear. The obstacle course requires recruits to cross lakes, streams, and bogs and pass through tunnels, one of which is completely submerged under water. Immediately after crossing the finish line, recruits move on to the thirty-meter rifle range, where they must register six hits in ten shots or repeat the entire course. The endurance course must be completed in seventy minutes or less.

Nine-mile speed march This test is a team effort. The recruits run in troop formation, each carrying full fighting gear, which includes a twenty-two-pound pack and a ten-pound rifle. The run must be completed in ninety minutes or less, and if one recruit fails, the entire troop fails.

Tarzan and assault course The Tarzan course is an aerial confidence test. Recruits must perform a "death slide" (rapid descent from a high plateau), complete an elevated ropes course, and scale a thirty-foot wall. The assault course features at least a dozen obstacles including a twelve-foot wall. Recruits are familiar with both courses, but this is the first time they complete the courses back-to-back, and they must do so in thirty minutes or less.

Thirty-mile load carry Again under the load of full fighting gear, the recruits must work as a team to navigate their way across the challenging hills and countryside of Dartmoor. The time limit for this thirty-mile "yomp" is eight hours.

Although the commando tests are daunting and deserving of their infamous reputation, the progressive nature of the training modules prepares the recruits for the challenge. Even if the recruit was in the worst physical condition on day one, if he was accepted as a Royal Marine recruit and stuck with the program through the twenty-five-week buildup, he would be equipped both physically and mentally to successfully complete the tests.

6. The Royal Marines Today

After World War II, the United States and the Soviet Union emerged as the world's military superpowers. Fundamental differences in the two governments led to fear and paranoia, however, culminating in the Cold War (1945–1991). The Cold War was a precarious global situation that would help to define the role of the Royal Marines for the next forty-five years.

Lines of loyalty were drawn at the beginning of the Cold War, and the United Kingdom joined the United States in the North Atlantic Treaty Organization (NATO). Royal Marines Commando units were uniquely trained to defend NATO's interests in the strategic stronghold of the

40 Commando in Afghanistan

On September 11, 2001, when terrorists using hijacked commercial airplanes attacked the United States, units from 40 Commando were undergoing a training exercise in Cyprus, Greece. As the exercise came to a close, England announced its involvement in the U.S.-led war against terrorism, and the commandos were immediately diverted to Afghanistan. These men were among the first British troops to enter the Afghan capital city of Kabul.

North Atlantic, and this became their primary assignment until the collapse of the Soviet Union in 1991.

Of course, the Royal Marines saw action in several other locations and conflicts around the world during this time, including the Korean War, the Falkland Islands War, Angola, and Grenada, but the Cold War influenced the responsibilities of the corps more than any other factor.

The end of the Cold War forced England to reevaluate its role in international affairs, leading to changes in its armed forces, including the Royal Marines Commandos. The organization that emerged is the special operations force that serves the interests of England today and is prepared to take immediate action in any emergency worldwide tomorrow.

Post–Cold War Deployment

Military experts originally believed the demise of the Soviet Union would mean cutbacks in special operations forces. This was because the enemy upon which England and the United States had concentrated so many resources defending against disappeared almost overnight. But the opposite has proven true. In the complex post–Cold War era, it is not always easy to identify enemies. It is even trickier to predict where the next threat will pop up. For these reasons, Royal Marines Commando units are more vital than ever.

Today, intelligence-gathering is a nation's best line of defense, and when a likely threat is identified, the strategy is to eliminate that danger at its source before it gains momentum. This is a tactic tailor-made for commando operations and has been exemplified by recent deployments. In 1994, commandos arrived in Kuwait to defend British

Brigidier Roger Lane *(right)* briefs Lieutenant-Colonel Mike Ellis *(center)* and Marine Chris Douglas *(left)*. The Royal Marines have joined U.S. troops on surveillance and reconnaissance missions in Afghanistan in the fight against terrorism.

interests against a small but potent invading Iraqi army; and currently, commandos find themselves in Afghanistan assisting the U.S.-led fight against the Al Qaeda terrorist network as well as providing humanitarian aid for Afghan refugees.

In the areas of infantry vehicles and weaponry, the trend has moved away from large tanks and heavy weapons, instead focusing on transport aircraft and vessels designed to deploy troops with quickness and precision.

Royal Marines examine arms they found in a raid of a barn in Afghanistan. Troops found weapons, plastic explosives, bomb-making equipment, and intelligence documents.

Looking Toward the Future

Exciting new developments constantly drive the advancement of the Royal Marines in directions inconceivable in past generations. On May 31, 2002, one such development occurred that literally changed the face of the corps. In her third and final attempt, Captain

The first woman to earn the Green Beret of a Royal Marines Commando, Captain Philippa Tattersall pulls herself along a rope to pass the All-Arms Commando Course at the Commando training center. Captain Tattersall may pave the way for the inclusion of women into the Royal Marines.

Philippa "Pip" Tattersall successfully completed the Tarzan and assault course and thirty-mile load carry to pass the final commando tests and become the first woman in history to earn the coveted Green Beret of a Royal Marines Commando.

Captain Tattersall's triumph forced British military leaders to reinforce their position against allowing women to participate in frontline combat operations. But with other women on Pip's heels, the floodgates may soon open to allow new opportunities for women within the Royal Marines. And a generation later, who is to say the inconceivable will not happen again?

As the British military stands today, the future emphasis of its armed forces is clearly to develop intelligence services and embrace new technologies to gather, process, and distribute information as rapidly as possible. The current crop of recruits is up to the test. Entering the corps with more education, computer skills, and technological savvy than previous recruits, the Royal Marines are facing opportunities—both inside and outside the military—that have never been greater. The result, however, is fewer career soldiers, and the corps is doing what it can to address this issue. By offering enormous technical training value, the Royal Marines continue to draw the best and brightest recruits. The corps

A Viking on the Horizon

In a move that will significantly increase the capacity of the corps, the Royal Marines plan to bring into service their first-ever armored vehicle in 2003. The Viking, like the commandos themselves, can operate anywhere in the world, on land or in water. Highly mobile and lightweight, the Viking goes where no other armored vehicle can and may be equipped with a heavy machine gun capable of engaging targets a mile away.

benefits by filling its ranks with quality commando candidates, and those who leave the service are equipped with valuable skills for the private sector.

The role of the Royal Marines Commandos is fast evolving in this increasingly digitized military environment; but with their combination of brain, brawn, and self-belief, it is clear this elite group of sea soldiers will continue to fight for freedom and international stability long into the twenty-first century.

Colonel Sam Basset might find the inner workings of the modern Royal Marines difficult to understand—and perhaps impossible to function within. However, the rich history of the corps remains and its tradition continues in the spirit of today's commandos. As Major Mike Norman explained to journalists during the Falkland Islands War, "Royal Marines don't surrender. It's not part of our training."

Glossary

admiralty The British government department that oversees the administrative affairs of the Royal Navy.

amphibious Referring to anything that is adapted for both land and water.

beachhead An initial position on an enemy shoreline captured by troops in advance of an invading force.

blitzkrieg A German word, which translates to "lightning war," blitzkrieg was used to describe the German army's method of sudden, swift, and relentless military assault.

cache A storage or hiding place, often for weapons.

camouflage The method of concealing military personnel or equipment from an enemy by making them appear to be part of the natural surroundings.

covert An undercover military operation that is planned and executed with the utmost secrecy in order to capitalize on the element of surprise.

coxswain   The person positioned at a boat's helm, responsible for steering the craft and commanding its crew.

deployment   The strategic and systematic placement of troops in battle formation in preparation for combat.

infantry   Soldiers armed and trained to fight on foot. Also, the units and military branches made up of these soldiers.

magazine   The chamber in a gun used for holding a number of cartridges or bullets to be fed automatically to the weapon for rapid firing and infrequent reloading.

maritime   Pertaining to the ocean or sea, including oceanic navigation, naval operations, and commerce by way of the sea.

module   A unit of education or instruction in which a single topic or a small section of a broad topic is studied for a given period of time.

mortar   A portable, muzzle-loading cannon used to fire explosive shells accurately at low velocities, short ranges, and high trajectories.

pass out   Graduation from CTCRM basic training, signifying a recruit has passed all the requirements necessary to join the ranks of the Royal Marines Commandos.

reconnaissance (recon)   An examination of a territory or of an enemy's position for the purpose of obtaining information necessary for directing military operations.

valor   Bravery.

For More Information

Ministry of Defence

The Ministerial Correspondence Unit

Room 222, Old War Office

Whitehall, London

SW1A 2EU

England

+44 870 607 4455

Web site: http://www.mod.uk

National Maritime Museum

Romney Road

Greenwich, London

SE10 9NF

England

+44 20 8858 4422

Web site: http://www.nmm.ac.uk

Royal Marines Museum

Southsea, Hampshire

PO4 9PX

England

+44 23 9281 9385

Web site: http://www.royalmarinesmuseum.co.uk

Royal Naval Museum

HM Naval Base (PP66)

Portsmouth, Hampshire

PO1 3NH

England

+44 23 9272 7562

Web site: http://www.royalnavalmuseum.org

Web Sites

Due to the changing nature of Internet links, the Rosen Publishing Group, Inc., has developed an online list of Web sites related to the subject of this book. This site is updated regularly. Please use this link to access the list:

http://www.rosenlinks.com/iso/brrm

For Further Reading

Brooks, Richard. *The Royal Marines: A History.* Annapolis, MD: Naval Institute Press, 2002.

Foster, Nigel. *The Making of a Royal Marine Commando.* London: Pan, 1988.

Ladd, James D. *Inside the Commandos.* Annapolis, MD: Naval Institute Press, 1984.

McNab, Chris. *Survive in the Arctic with the Royal Marine Commando.* Broomall, PA: Mason Crest Publishers, 2002.

Vaux, Nick F. *Take That Hill!: Royal Marines in the Falklands.* Washington, DC: Pergamon-Brassey's International Defense Publishers, Inc., 1987.

Young, Peter. *Storm from the Sea.* Annapolis, MD: Naval Institute Press, 1989.

Bibliography

Basset, Samuel John Woodruff. *Royal Marine*. New York: Stein and Day, 1965.

BBC News. "UK's Mountain Warfare Elite." March 2002. Retrieved May 2002 (http://news.bbc.co.uk/1/hi/uk/1593996.stm).

Beaver, Paul. *Encyclopedia of the Modern Royal Navy Including the Fleet Air Arm and Royal Marines*. Rev. ed. Wellingborough, Northants, England: Patrick Stephens Limited, 1985.

Emuang, Keith. "The Royal Marines—From Past to Present." February 2002. Retrieved April 2002 (http://content.miw.com.sg/LifeStyle/Military/ls_military01_20020218.asp).

Lloyd, Mark. *Modern Combat Uniforms*. Carrollton, TX: Squadron/Signal Publications Inc., 1988.

Preston, Antony, ed. *History of the Royal Navy in the 20th Century*. Novato, CA: Presidio Press, 1987.

Index

H
helicopters, 23, 34, 37, 39
HMS *Bulwark*, 23
Hong Kong, 15, 20
humanitarian assistance, 24, 25

I
intelligence gathering, 51
Iraq, 21, 24, 42
Israel, 20

K
Kuwait, 23, 51
Korean War, 23, 28, 50

L
landing craft, 17, 31–32, 34, 37–39
Lebanon crisis, 23
lord high admiral, 8, 11

M
modules, 42–46, 48
Mountain and Arctic Warfare Cadre
(M&AW) 27, 29–31, 34

N
North Atlantic Treaty Organization
(NATO), 24, 29, 49
Normandy, 17, 31
Norway, 21, 23–24, 29–30

O
operational performance standard
(OPS), 42

P
Potential Royal Marines Course
(PRMC), 42

R
raiding missions, 27
reconnaissance (recon), 29, 44
recruits, 5, 6, 11, 17, 29, 41–48, 54
Royal Air Force, 26
Royal Fleet Auxiliary, 26
Royal Navy, 8, 10–12, 15–16, 23, 26,
31–32, 34

S
Seven Years' War, 15
Soviet Union, 49–51
Spanish Armada, 12
Special Air Service (SAS), 29
Special Boat Squadron (SBS), 27–29
special operations (special ops) force,
6–7, 9, 50–51
Suez crisis, 23

T
Tarzan Course, 47, 53
Tattersall, Captain Philippa "Pip," 52–53
technology, 7, 27, 31, 34, 54
3 Commando Brigade Royal Marines
(3 Cdo Bde RM), 18–19, 22,
24–25, 26, 28, 29, 33
tradition, 7, 55
training, 6, 7, 17, 19, 24, 27, 35,
41, 43
troops, 12, 17, 18–19, 21, 30, 32, 33,
37–39, 43, 47, 52
29 Commando, 28

W
weaponry, 9, 31, 34, 35–37, 52
World War I, 15
World War II, 7, 15, 17, 18–20, 23,
27, 49

About the Author

A writer/historian with a bachelor's degree in American and modern European history, Bill Scheppler has written on topics from the Ironman to the Internet—and now, the British Royal Marines.

Credits

Cover, p. 1 © Peter Russell/The Military Picture Library/Corbis; pp. 4, 21, 52, 53 © AP/Wide World Photos; p. 13 © Hulton/Archive/Getty Images; p. 14 © Stapleton Collection/Corbis; p. 16 © Timepix; p. 20 © Bettmann/Corbis; pp. 24, 30 © Robin Adshead/The Military Picture Library/Corbis; pp. 38, 39, 45, 51 © Reuters New Media Inc./Corbis.

Editor

Christine Poolos

Design and Layout

Les Kanturek